TAKAYA'S JOURNEY

Cheryl Alexander and Jenaya Copithorne

RMB

For my grandchildren, Dana, Elliott, Lila, Mira and Reni.
Like Takaya, you are unique and inspire.

Takaya, the young wolf, is wild and free.
He loves to explore and to swim in the sea.
For two years, he lives, hunts, and plays in a pack,
Until a time comes when he has to make tracks.

After some time, when Takaya is grown,

He's ready to start a new pack of his own.

He's off on a journey, he's ready to roam.

He wanders in search of a mate and a home.

His journey through forests and cities is long,
But Takaya is smart and Takaya is strong.
He dreams about what kind of life will await:
A safe home with food, and maybe a mate!

Courageous Takaya keeps walking for weeks,
Then finally he sees the new home that he seeks:
A group of small islands, all covered in trees,
With tall rocky bluffs overlooking the sea.

He swims to one island, climbs onto the shore,
And wanders up into the woods to explore.
The island is beautiful, wild as could be.

Eagles soar in the sky.

Orcas splash in the sea.

This is a good place for a lone wolf to rest,
He curls up secure in a green mossy nest.
He dreams of the creatures he hunted last year:
Some elk and some beaver, but usually deer.

Takaya goes searching for some kind of prey,
He wanders each path and explores every bay.
He finds lots of critters, some big and some small,
There's no elk or beaver, and no deer at all.

After searching the islands, it soon becomes clear:
He's alone in this place, there are no wolves here.
Takaya had hoped to find friends and a mate.
He'll have to keep looking – or just stay and wait.

Discouraged, Takaya sits down and he sighs.
But then he jumps up with a "Woof!" of surprise.
Down on the water, right under his snout,
A human is splashing and paddling about.

Takaya decides he will not linger here,
So close to the humans, so far from the deer.
He goes back to the sea and starts swimming away,
Hoping to find somewhere better to stay.

He swims through cold waters, setting his sights
On a small rocky island all bright with white lights.
Perhaps there's a chance that this island could be
A home for a young wolf adrift in the sea.

He reaches the island, but all that he sees
Is bare rocky ground, with no prey and no trees.
Takaya will have to continue his quest.
He jumps in the water and starts swimming west.

But once in the water, he hears a low sound:
A rumbling noise that makes his heart pound.
He sees a boat speeding his way with a roar.
Takaya is scared, and he swims back to shore.

Takaya is tired and frightened and cold.

He doesn't feel brave and he doesn't feel bold.

He thinks of his cozy bed, soft and moss-lined,

On the beautiful island he left far behind.

Takaya decides to swim back to the shore
Of the islands he'd visited just days before.
He climbs on the rocks, and he shakes himself dry,
And trots off to explore under soft coastal skies.

The first thing he needs is a good healthy meal,
So, Takaya decides to try catching a seal.
It's really quite yummy, much better than deer.
Takaya is happy. He thinks he'll stay here.

One day he hears noises that echo and grow,
He peeks through the trees to see people below.
He hides in the grass and gives them some space.
Takaya and humans could both share this place.

Takaya is learning all kinds of new things:
He hunts sneaky otters and geese with strong wings.

He digs for fresh water when ponds are all dry.
He even gives rocky shore fishing a try.

Takaya is now in an excellent mood.

He's found a safe home and he's found some good food.

He still hopes that one day he will find a mate.

Takaya is patient and willing to wait.

For now he is happy to wander alone.
Takaya is brave and can live on his own.

Takaya has all that he needs to survive.
Takaya adapts and he learns how to thrive.

He loves his new home and so here he will stay,
Content to explore and to wander each day.
He howls every evening at the setting sun,
Glad that for now, his journey is done.

TEACHER & PARENT RESOURCES

1. How is Takaya different from most other wolves?

2. Takaya lives alone. Who do you live with?

3. Takaya is a special wolf. What makes you special?

4. Why do you think Takaya left his family (his pack)?

5. What challenges do you think Takaya faced during his journey to the islands?

6. Wolves need certain things to be well and happy. What do you think Takaya needs?

7. Do you think Takaya found a safe home? He loves his home. What is your home like?

8. Why do you think it would be difficult for Takaya to live so close to humans?
How do you think Takaya has adapted to living so close to humans?

9. Why did Takaya have to learn new things in his islands? What did he learn?

10. Takaya's fur blends into his environment. How do you think this helps him to survive?

11. Takaya ate new foods while in the islands. What new foods have you tried?

12. What are some reasons why Takaya might howl?

13. What kinds of animals kept Takaya company? Who keeps you company?

14. Takaya has a good life on the island, but still wants to find a mate.
What will make it hard for him to find a mate?

15. What can people learn from Takaya's story?

For information on purchasing bulk quantities of this book, or to obtain media excerpts or invite the authors to speak at an event, please visit rmbooks.com and select the "Contact" tab.

RMB | Rocky Mountain Books Ltd.
rmbooks.com
@rmbooks
facebook.com/rmbooks

Cataloguing data available from Library and Archives Canada
ISBN 9781771604895 (hardcover)
ISBN 9781771604901 (softcover)
ISBN 9781771604918 (electronic)

Printed and bound in China

We would like to also take this opportunity to acknowledge the traditional territories upon which we live and work. In Calgary, Alberta, we acknowledge the Niitsítapi (Blackfoot) and the people of the Treaty 7 region in Southern Alberta, which includes the Siksika, the Piikuni, the Kainai, the Tsuut'ina, and the Stoney Nakoda First Nations, including Chiniki, Bearpaw, and Wesley First Nations. The City of Calgary is also home to Métis Nation of Alberta, Region III. In Victoria, British Columbia, we acknowledge the traditional territories of the Lkwungen (Esquimalt and Songhees), Malahat, Pacheedaht, Scia'new, T'Sou-ke, and W̱SÁNEĆ (Pauquachin, Tsartlip, Tsawout, Tseycum) peoples.

We acknowledge the financial support of the Government of Canada through the Canada Book Fund and the Canada Council for the Arts, and of the province of British Columbia through the British Columbia Arts Council and the Book Publishing Tax Credit.